Gullah Ghosts

Also by Lynn Michelsohn

Lowcountry Ghosts

Tales from Brookgreen
Folklore, Ghost Stories, and Gullah Folktales in the
South Carolina Lowcountry

In the Galapagos Islands
with Herman Melville

Roswell
Your Travel Guide to the UFO Capital of the World!

Billy the Kid's Jail
Santa Fe, New Mexico

Gullah Ghosts

Stories and Folktales
from
Brookgreen Gardens
in the
South Carolina Lowcountry
with
Notes on Gullah Culture and History

by
Lynn Michelsohn

Cleanan Press
Roswell, NM USA

Gullah Ghosts
Stories and Folktales from Brookgreen Gardens
in the South Carolina Lowcountry with Notes
on Gullah Culture and History

Print Edition 1.0 CS (9/13)

An ebook edition is also available.

Images used with permission are from photographs by Welden Bayliss (pp 14, 83), Moses Michelsohn (p 31), and Aaron Michelsohn (pp 13, 20, 42). All other illustrations are by the author.

Published by:
    Cleanan Press, Inc.
    106 North Washington Avenue
    Roswell, NM 88203 USA

    www.cleananpress.com

Acknowledgements

The youthful delight that Moses expressed at hearing these stories reminded me of my own enthusiasm for them. Aaron, ever the editor, guided me in writing them down. Alice Duncan typed and retyped. Larry supported this and all my "family stuff." My parents gave me their love and support always. Honey's Horry heritage and Daddy's interest in "local color" shaped my love of the Carolina Lowcountry.

Genevieve Chandler Peterkin encouraged me to recall these stories from my early visits to Brookgreen.

The kind hospitality of Mary Emily and Nelson Jackson II repeatedly brought me back to South Carolina. Their daughter Kaki shared her own recollections of our Cousin Corrie's interest in the supernatural with me.

Helen Benso, Vice President of Marketing at Brookgreen Gardens, assisted with this project in several ways including obtaining permission to use materials, correcting factual errors, and providing encouragement.

Most importantly, Cousin Corrie and Miss Genevieve told the tales recorded on these pages. I thank them for sharing their wonderful stories of Brookgreen with all of us who love the Carolina Lowcountry.

Table of Contents

Preface

Chapter 1.   11
A Cultural Note: The Gullah Language

Chapter 2.   15
Crab Boy's Ghost

Chapter 3.   21
Don't Tief!

Chapter 4.   33
A Historical Note: Class Leaders,
Parson Belin, and the
Methodist Mission to the Slaves

Chapter 5.   43
The Great Sandy Island Expedition

Chapter 6.   61
A Historical Note: Phillip Washington,
Sandy Island Community Organizer

About the Storytellers: The Hostesses   69
of Brookgreen Gardens

A Selection from *Lowcountry Ghosts*   *77*

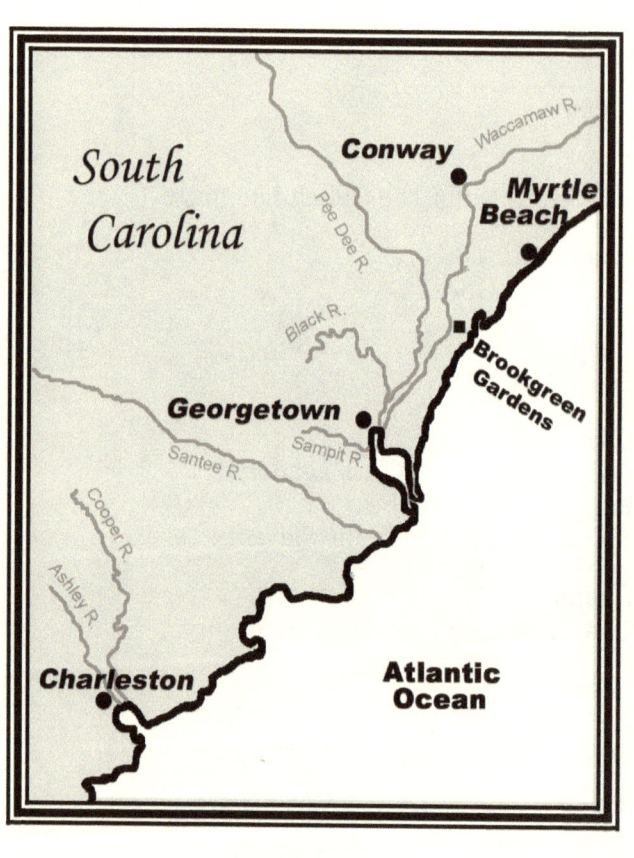

Preface

These are some of the stories told by Miss Genevieve and Cousin Corrie, two charming Hostesses at Brookgreen Gardens in the South Carolina Lowcountry during the middle of the Twentieth Century (described in the chapter, About the Storytellers: The Hostesses of Brookgreen Gardens). They are excerpted from my longer work, *Tales from Brookgreen: Folklore, Ghost Stories, and Gullah Folktales from the South Carolina Lowcountry*. I hope you enjoy them.

Lynn Michelsohn

Chapter 1.
A Cultural Note:
The Gullah Language

Miss Genevieve, one of the Hostesses at Brookgreen Gardens in the mid-Twentieth Century, explained the development of the Gullah language spoken by descendents of slaves in the South Carolina Lowcountry like this . . .

Nobody can tell you for sure how the Gullah language developed but people who have studied it do have some idea about its history and this is how they explain it.

Slaves brought to South Carolina came from different parts of West Africa. Each African area and tribal group had its own language and customs. When slaves arrived on Lowcountry plantations, communication was a big challenge. Slaves and planters spoke different languages and often, fellow slaves even spoke different languages yet all had to understand each other well enough to live and work together.

A pidgin language developed that contained words and grammatical structures from English and from various African languages. Planters and overseers kept speaking English and slaves kept speaking their own various languages but each also learned to speak the pidgin language, called Gullah, to communicate with each other. People who study languages tell me that at this stage Gullah was a pidgin language because no one spoke it as his native language but those speaking different languages used it to communicate with each other. Some people think the name Gullah came from the word Angola, which was the homeland of many of the slaves.

As new generations of slaves were born in the Lowcountry, these children grew up speaking Gullah as their native language. Gullah became a creole language, which is one whose words and grammar are a combination of different languages but one which is now the native language of a group of people, in this case, the descendants of the slaves brought from Africa.

Planters and other whites continued to speak English, of course, but also spoke Gullah to communicate with their workers. Planters and their families often learned Gullah as children from nurses and other household servants who helped raise them.

Chapter 2.
Crab Boy's Ghost

Cousin Corrie loved ghost stories and anything related to the supernatural, from ancient Egyptian tales of the mystical powers of cats to present-day theories of ESP. She often entertained teenage cousins with "table turning," an old-fashioned group activity designed to contact the spirit world. Like many in the Lowcountry, Cousin Corrie had grown up accepting the spirit world as just another aspect of reality, whether this spirit world was based on religious beliefs preached from the Sunday pulpit or on the folklore of haunts, hags, and plat-eyes that she learned from her Gullah family servants. The story of Crab Boy was one she heard as a child in her home at Woodlawn, on the creek at Murrells Inlet. She especially liked telling it to children.

When I was a child we lived in a big wooden house right on the seashore at Murrells Inlet.

Sometimes, early in the morning we would hear faint but urgent screams coming over and over from far down the creek toward Drunken Jack Island, behind what is now Huntington Beach. My mother, who didn't stand for any such nonsense, always said it was just a peacock calling from a distant farmyard. But the Gullah women who helped my mother in the kitchen told us children that it was the ghost of Crab Boy crying for help. They called such spirits of children who had died unnatural deaths "drolls."

Saltwater creeks and marshes between sandy barrier islands like Huntington Beach and the mainland seashore are full of sea life. This sea life becomes delicious seafood for those who know how to catch it. As children, my brothers and sisters and I caught fish, raked oysters, and dug for clams. My father and brothers caught shrimp in hand thrown nets. We easily attracted blue crabs with a fish head tied to a length of twine as they swam in on the rising tide. Once a crab was feeding, we pulled the fish head in slowly until the crab was close enough to "swoop" it up with a dip net. Sometimes we would see crabs just resting along the water's edge and could scoop them up without even needing fish heads.

Oysters, blue crabs, and clams all make delicious eating but the greatest delicacy of the marsh is the stone crab, with sweet juicy meat in its giant claw. Catching stone crabs requires a very different technique than catching blue crabs

16

however. Stone crabs do not swim in and out with the tide. They live deep in burrows in the mud banks along the creeks. The burrows are only exposed at low tide. Catching a stone crab requires a highly skilled technique and a lot of courage. That giant claw that is so delicious to eat can crush a finger with little effort.

The best way to catch a stone crab is to wait for low tide, then walk along the edge of the creek looking for stone crab burrows. When you see one, which is just about as big around as your fist, you slowly slide your hand and arm way into it until you feel the crab with your fingers. Then you gently grab the crab "just the right way" and slip it out of the burrow and into your bucket. If the crab senses danger it will wedge itself in its hole with its legs and shell and attack with that giant claw.

Now this method of catching stone crabs has been carefully explained to me, don't you understand? I would never try it myself. Not after growing up hearing stories of Crab Boy!

No one ever seemed to know Crab Boy's real name. He wasn't from around these parts. He came down to stay with relatives that lived here at Murrells Inlet near the shore behind Drunken Jack Island on land that is now part of Brookgreen Gardens. Before Freedom, Crab Boy's uncles had all been slaves here on the Waccamaw Neck on Brookgreen Plantation, or was it at The Oaks? Anyway, their job had been to provide all kinds of seafood for their planter's table. Then after

Freedom, they remained at Murrells Inlet living off the bounty of its creeks and marshes.

Crab Boy's uncles and cousins caught all manner of seafood that they sold to the people living in cottages from Magnolia Beach all the way to the north end of Murrells Inlet at Sunnyside. Stone crab claws brought the most money but stone crabs took patience and skill to catch.

Crab Boy's relatives took him along as they gathered their harvest from the creeks. He learned to cast a shrimp net and to gather oysters carefully so as not to cut himself on their razor sharp shells. However his uncles warned him repeatedly, "Never go after stone crabs the way we do until you are much older."

Did he listen? Of course not!

One day when the tide was just past its low point Crab Boy was exploring the maze of creeks by himself when he saw a perfect stone crab hole. He had seen his uncles pull crabs out so easily that he was sure he could do it too.

The boy crouched down to the thick dark mud surrounding the hole and slowly reached in farther and farther until nearly his whole arm was extended into the burrow. Finally his fingers contacted the hard sharp creature. As he tried to slide his hand under the shell, the crab grabbed his finger with its crushing grip.

Crab Boy shrieked in pain! He tried to yank his arm out of the hole but it wouldn't budge! The

Chapter 2

crab had wedged itself solidly in the burrow and would not release its grip on the boy's finger.

Crab Boy screamed louder and louder for help. His uncles heard the cries and began searching for him but in the maze of creeks and marshes his calls seemed to come from every direction! His frantic relatives searched and searched until the rising tide stilled his voice. They found Crab Boy's lifeless body at the next low tide, his arm still trapped in the stone crab's burrow.

As a child I always wondered how they ever got his arm out so they could bury Crab Boy. Nobody ever answered that question for me. But whenever we children went out into the marsh they always reminded us to leave stone crabs alone. And whenever we heard the droll shrieking from down toward Drunken Jack Island they told us the story of Crab Boy.

Now even though these stories frightened us, they probably served a useful purpose: to keep us children from fooling around in the mud and putting our hands where they didn't belong. And they certainly worked for me! To this day I won't reach my hand into any hole in the creek bank.

The local people say Mrs. Chandler, here, is the only white woman in Murrells Inlet who can catch stone crabs. She can, too! I think it's because she didn't live here at the Inlet when she was little so she didn't hear the stories about Crab Boy until she was older. Those of us who did are just too scared to try!

Chapter 3.
Don't Tief!

Cousin Corrie occasionally recounted stories that old "Dr. Wardie," beloved physician of Brookgreen Plantation had told her many years previously. This was a story Dr. Wardie had heard from his aunt, "Miss Bessie." He, Cousin Corrie, and Miss Bessie all enjoyed the story because it revealed that high and mighty rice planters of olden times didn't always have everything their own way.

Although the rice harvest was bountiful that year in the mid-1800s on Brookgreen Plantation the plantation Overseer was troubled. The yield in rice didn't seem to be as large as he had expected. The Overseer thought and thought about this and finally became convinced that someone was stealing rice from the barn where they stored it after threshing.

But who could be taking the rice, and how? No one could steal rice during the day with so many people about, yet how could anyone get into the rice barn at night? It was locked carefully each evening and there were no signs of break-in.

Suddenly the Overseer realized who locked the barn each evening! Devine, the head slave on the plantation, held the keys. Old stories began to recall themselves to the Overseer, stories about Devine stealing rice and selling it to buy liquor (and of how Devine had gotten caught but I won't go into that right now).

"So!" mused the Overseer to himself, "Devine is sneaking into the barn at night and stealing rice again! And he is probably bringing other slaves with him because a lot of rice seemed to be missing. Now how can I catch Devine and his accomplices in their act of thievery?"

The Overseer thought, and thought some more, and finally devised a plan. He would hide in the rice barn at night and surprise Devine when he and the others came in to steal rice. And he would put his plan into effect that very evening!

After the day's work was completed the workers all went home to the Street, as the community of slave cabins was called. The Overseer also went home to his cottage near the Street but after dark he crept back to the rice barn, which was located where the Dogwood Garden stands today at Brookgreen Gardens, just behind us here in the Museum. The Overseer looked around stealthily but all was still. He unlocked the door, slipped into the barn, and carefully relocked the door from the inside.

The rice barn was not a very inviting place to spend the night but the Overseer made himself a pallet out of rice straw and curled up near the door to wait. He didn't bother to stay awake because he knew that anyone entering the barn would rouse him.

The next morning the Overseer awoke nicely rested. His sleep had not been disturbed by anyone coming into the barn. Disappointed but undaunted, he slept in the barn again the next night, with the same results.

This puzzled the Overseer greatly. Why wasn't his plan working? He thought some more and decided that Devine must have known somehow that he was sleeping in the rice barn. Of course Devine and the others would avoid coming in to steal rice with him there. So, that evening the Overseer made a big show of moving his pallet out of the barn and giving up his attempt to catch anyone coming into the barn at night. But as soon as it was dark he sneaked out of his cottage and crept back to the rice barn. This time he hid himself in the trees along the edge of the barnyard where he could keep close watch on the barn without being seen.

The Overseer sat for hours watching in the dark, again with no results. No moon or stars shone through the cloudy skies and night noises made him uneasy at times but he was determined to catch his thief.

Suddenly a faint light appeared at the far edge of the barnyard. The Overseer's initial thrill quickly turned to apprehension. This was a very strange looking light. It was not a torch but a faint, eerie glow. Gradually his apprehension turned to terror. All the stories he had ever heard about haunts and plat eyes came rushing back to him as the faint glow bobbed slowly along the far tree line. What manner of horrifying specter was coming from the miasmic swamps to threaten him? At least it wasn't coming any closer!

Slowly the glow moved toward one of the outbuildings in the barnyard, the one where workers stored rice straw after they threshed the rice grains out of it. Nothing was wasted on the plantation and even worthless rice straw made good animal bedding or compost for cornfields.

In another moment, a light flared inside the outbuilding as if someone had lit a torch. Suddenly the explanation came to the shaken Overseer: the faint glow that he had watched bob along the tree line had come from a glowing ember carried hidden in a pot. Now someone had used that ember to light a torch inside the building.

Fear drained from the Overseer to be replaced by curiosity. What was anyone doing sneaking into the shed where they stored rice straw? The Overseer moved closer until he could see inside the building. A large muscular slave

Chapter 3

stood with his back to the doorway holding a small "fat light'erd," a splinter of pine heartwood saturated with pine resin that served as a torch, illuminating the inside of the building. Under his direction three field hands dug down into the piles of straw and pulled out seagrass baskets. From the baskets they poured rice into sacks.

When the sacks were full and tied closed the workers hoisted them over their shoulders. The man with the torch then turned to lead them out and the Overseer could see him clearly. It was not Devine. It was John! One of Captain Ward's most trusted field hands, and the plantation Class Leader!

As the Overseer watched, John extinguished his torch. He and the others stole back out into the night and headed toward their homes in the Street. The Overseer understood that later they would pound the rice in homemade mortars hidden in the swamps to remove the outer hulls, then boil it up for dinner in their cabins in the Street. Not only would they have extra rice to stretch their weekly rations, but fancy whole grain rice even better than the midlins, which are the broken grains that could not be sold on the international market, that Captain Ward and his family ate, and certainly better than the small broken pieces the slaves usually got in their weekly food ration.

Now the whole situation became clear. No wonder he hadn't caught his rice thief by sleeping in the barn. Devine was not stealing rice from the barn. Nobody was stealing rice from the barn! And Devine was not involved at all. The thief was John!

Each day as field workers threshed the rice and scooped it into baskets, they hid some of the baskets in bundles of straw instead of taking them to the rice barn. Then when they carried the bundles of rice straw into the outbuilding for storage they were also carrying away hidden baskets of the newly threshed grain. Later they easily returned during the night to collect the hidden rice from under the straw in the unlocked shed. There was no need to steal rice from the carefully locked rice barn!

The Overseer had discovered his thieves at last. And the biggest shock was that John, the plantation Class Leader—the supposedly pious slave religious leader—was now leading them in their thievery!

Captain Ward had grown to admire John, the Class Leader on his Brookgreen Plantation. John was a tall strong man, a good worker, and a leader among his people. As a field hand, he became expert in all phases of rice production. Captain Ward came to rely on John more and more because of his intelligence, his expertise, his leadership abilities, and especially because of his honesty.

The plantation Overseer was not quite so trusting of John and sometimes resented Captain Ward's reliance on John's judgment in matters related to the rice growing operation. But Captain

Chapter 3

Ward continued to entrust John with numerous responsibilities and to praise his abilities and his loyalty.

The year that this story took place, which must have been shortly before the War, had been a good one for rice production. When the harvest came, Captain Ward placed John in charge of the threshing floor just in front of the rice barn. John worked under the direction of Devine, the Driver or head slave, and under the direction of the white Overseer of course, but Captain Ward trusted John completely and gave him serious responsibilities. After all, John was the Class Leader on Brookgreen Plantation.

The harvest was in full swing. Every day rice flats piled high with bundles of rice stalks laden with plump grains of rice arrived at Brookgreen Landing, just down the rice island steps from us here at the Museum. A steady stream of field hands carried bundles of rice stalks up the steps from flatboats to the barnyard. John directed them as they arranged the bundles on the hard packed dirt of the threshing floor in front of the barn.

Under John's supervision, workers beat the rice stalks with wooden flails to knock rice grains loose from the stalks. Then, they scooped up the rough rice from the threshing floor into coiled seagrass baskets and carried it into the rice barn to storage bins where it would wait for milling later in the season. Finally, they carried off the bundles of rice stalks, now just the remaining straw, to an outbuilding for storage.

At least, that was what was supposed to happen. But now, the Overseer had discovered that John wasn't sending all the rice into the barn. There in the dark of the midnight barnyard the Overseer had discovered the secret of John's unimagined thievery!

~ ~ ~

The Overseer was eager to tell Captain Ward what he had discovered, especially since it involved John, whom he had long suspected of being less perfect than Captain Ward believed. The Overseer went to Captain Ward first thing the next morning and recounted his story.

Captain Ward was a strict man but he was fair. When his Overseer came to him with the story of John leading other field hands in stealing rice, Captain Ward determined to give John a chance to defend himself against the charge. Stealing was a serious offense that merited severe punishment.

Captain Ward sent for John. There on the front porch of the plantation mansion that stood where the Alligator Bender Pool stands today, in the presence of the Ward family, the household servants, and the Overseer, Captain Ward confronted his trusted Class Leader.

"John, are you a good Christian man?"

"I most certainly am, Master Josh, sir!" John replied with enthusiasm.

Chapter 3

Captain Ward agreed and went on to praise John's leadership and his fine record of behavior and hard work at Brookgreen. Then he grew more solemn.

"John, I need to ask you about something and I'm sure you will tell me the truth. You know it is a sin to lie."

"Most certainly, Master Josh, sir," John agreed.

Captain Ward went on to detail the Overseer's charges. He concluded with a direct question, "John, are you stealing my rice?"

Shocked, John drew himself up to his full height and looked Captain Ward straight in the eye.

"Stealing! I am not stealing!" His exact words, in the Gullah language that he had spoken all his life, were "Tief! Ah don't tief!"

"Master Josh, sir," John went on to explain, "The rice is your property, isn't it, sir?"

To this Captain Ward readily agreed.

"And I am your property, and all of us slaves are your property, aren't we, sir?"

Again, Captain Ward agreed.

"Now how is it stealing?" John asked, staring earnestly at his master. "When we move your rice from your barnyard into your slaves, we are just moving one property into another property. You haven't lost any property. It's still your rice and your slaves."

Captain Ward stared at John but had no answer for him.

Miss Bessie, Captain Ward's wife, spoke up quickly in support of John. "That's right!" she proclaimed emphatically with an amused smile, "My rice, my slaves!"

Captain Ward was never sure whether John was too clever for him in his use of words, or whether John was truly sincere in his understanding of the economics of the situation. Either way, Captain Ward felt compelled to forego any punishment for taking the rice. However, in the future he did keep a much closer eye on his most trusted worker: John, the Class Leader of Brookgreen Plantation!

That wasn't quite the end of the story though. In front of the whole group gathered there on the porch that morning, Miss Bessie went on to insist that if workers were taking extra rice, it was because they weren't getting enough to eat. With another smile she ordered the Overseer to increase their weekly ration.

And over the years Miss Bessie always broke into that same smile as she recalled Captain Ward's consternation on the mansion porch that morning.

"My rice, my slaves!" she always repeated, chuckling to herself whenever she told the story, as she often did in years to come.

"My rice, my slaves!"

Chapter 4.
A Historical Note:
Class Leaders, Parson
Belin, and the Methodist
Mission to the Slaves

Now I should tell you something about what it meant to be a Class Leader and why it was so shocking that a Class Leader would be involved in stealing.

For you to really understand about Class Leaders I have to explain about the Methodist Mission to the Slaves on the Waccamaw Neck. That all started with Parson James Lynch Belin (which he pronounced "Blane"), who was a great-uncle of Dr. Wardie, the man who told me this story.

James Belin grew up in Charleston in a wealthy planter family. Like all planters' sons he was educated for life as a planter himself. His older brother, Allard Belin, enjoyed the politics and mercantile dealing that made up a planter's life but James did not, although he accepted the vocation that his family had planned for him.

When James reached adulthood in the early 1800s, his father gave him the management, and later the ownership, of Wachesaw Plantation here on the Waccamaw Neck (we don't know the exact details, thanks to General Sherman, but that's another story). James was quite content to move to the Waccamaw Neck. He had always preferred the quiet isolated lifestyle of planters here to the social whirl and political intrigues in Georgetown and Charleston that so engaged his older brother.

Additionally, James' favorite sister, Margaret, and her husband, Dr. Ebenezer Flagg, made their home here. Dr. Eben, as he was known, was the son of Dr. Henry Flagg and Rachel Moore Allston Flagg of Brookgreen Plantation (remember them?). Dr. Eben had not inherited any land on the Waccamaw Neck but he contracted his medical services to other planters to take care of their families and their large populations of slaves.

Because of their close proximity and compatibility, James grew especially attached to Eben and Margaret and to their growing family. He never had children and soon came to view the Flagg children almost as his own. He shared Eben and Margaret's joy at the birth of each child, and then their sorrow at the early death of their first born son, Allard Belin Flagg, named in honor of

Chapter 4

Margaret and James' successful brother Allard (perhaps in the hope that wealthy Brother Allard would become a patron to his namesake, as was often the custom at that time).

When Eben and Margaret had another son, James encouraged them to name him Allard Belin Flagg II, in remembrance of their beloved firstborn as well as their successful brother. James enjoyed the other Flagg children, including Arthur and Alice, but always took a special interest in Allard and even gave him Wachesaw Plantation when he became an adult.

Of course, like most planters, James Belin had been raised in the Episcopal Church. Like many in the Carolina Lowcountry in the early 1800s however, he was curious about early Methodist bishops who traveled these wild areas by horseback, holding camp meetings and revivals where they expounded fiery new doctrines that challenged established teachings of the Episcopal Church. He heard both Bishop Asbury and Bishop Coke preach in their travels through the Lowcountry. James soon "caught the spark of this new fire." He traveled to hear Methodist preaching as often as he could and decided to dedicate his life to spreading the Word of God as Methodists understood it to be. Bishop Asbury himself ordained James Belin as a Methodist minister.

Now Methodism had run into one major stumbling block in South Carolina. Basic tenets of Methodism held that slavery was wrong. You can imagine that this teaching did not sit too well with the powers that be, most of whom were large slave owners. It was bad enough having to deal with Northern abolitionists but now to have charismatic preachers traveling throughout the countryside teaching that God's Word spoke against the very institution that formed the basis for their whole way of life was just too much! Wealthy and powerful planters began to oppose this new religion with vigor.

Methodist bishops soon recognized that practical considerations demanded a change in Church policy. Using logic along the lines of "Render unto Caesar what is Caesar's," the Methodist Church decided that in areas where the law sanctioned slavery, they would not press this issue.

Perhaps as a way to soothe their consciences, Church leaders established a Methodist Mission to the Slaves that rapidly gained support in the Carolina Lowcountry as well as in other Southern states.

This Mission gave slaves in the American South the same chance to receive the benefits of God's Word and the teachings of Christ that Methodist Missions to Africa and China gave other non-Christians.

Before the early 1800s, nobody had paid much attention to the religion of slaves who worked the plantations. Most slaves had brought their tribal religions with them from Africa, of course, and still practiced them as far as possible in their new circumstances. Planters suppressed practices that they considered blatantly heathen but most African practices and beliefs remained strong, if hidden, and many still do today. The whole subject of Hoodoo and conjure doctors and protective spells and evil spirits is one that outside people know very little about.

Many slaves readily accepted the new Christian religion when it was offered to them. That is not to say that they necessarily gave up their old religions but this new one seemed a good addition to deal with their concerns in America, and it did offer hope of a better life to come in the Promised Land, a land where all toils and tasks were over.

So James Belin became a Methodist preacher and he found all the work he would ever need right around him. He continued to operate his Wachesaw Plantation but devoted himself to the Methodist Church's Mission to the Slaves on the Waccamaw Neck.

At first Parson Belin's neighbors were shocked by the idea of his mission. At times they actively discouraged his efforts so he started out preaching only to his own slaves on Wachesaw Plantation. He was soon able to convince Robert and Francis Withers, who by that time owned nearby Brookgreen and Springfield Plantations, to let him minister to their slaves as well.

On Sundays, always a day of rest on plantations, Parson Belin preached the Gospel to slaves gathered outdoors under the shade of spreading live oak boughs. He held catechism classes for adults and children where he taught them to recite the questions and answers of Methodist doctrine from memory. But more was needed. In those days, joining the Methodist Church was not a simple matter. The Methodist Church required serious study and a period of probation for prospective members before baptism and being admitted to "the Communion of Saints, the Forgiveness of Sins, the Resurrection of the Body, and the Life Everlasting." Parson Belin could not do all the teaching himself so he selected a slave from each plantation who could read and write at least a little to become the Class Leader. Under Parson Belin's instruction, Class Leaders read and studied the Bible and other religious tracts, then taught their fellow slaves what they had learned. In this way Class Leaders prepared their class members to be baptized and to join the Methodist Church.

Becoming a Class Leader was quite an honor. It was also a way to gain special privileges among plantation slaves. Only the most intelligent, educated, diligent, and outwardly moral were selected for this great honor and position of trust. Each worked hard to maintain himself as a model of pious devotion to the tenets of Christianity. And each led the constant effort to seek out and severely chastise anyone in the slave community whose behavior might be unacceptable in the eyes of God, or the plantation master. The Class Leader became the paragon, as well as the enforcer, of moral righteousness on each plantation.

Parson Belin made a good start in the early years of his Mission to the Slaves, but then the Vesey Rebellion, a thwarted slave uprising in Charleston in 1822, brought the Mission to the Slaves to a standstill.

Planters throughout the Lowcountry began to oppose the Mission because they believed that instruction and organization by slave Class Leaders had encouraged the Vesey Rebellion. Hysteria of all sorts took hold. In spite of this Parson Belin continued his work.

Finally, after the furor had died down, more planters began to recognize the benefits of the Mission to the Slaves. In addition to any concerns they might have had for their slaves' spiritual welfare, planters began to see practical advantages in teaching them the Christian Gospel. In the planters' eyes these teachings promoted stability on the plantation by encouraging order, obedience, and morality among slaves and by reducing lawlessness and the most obvious vices.

In fact, in addition to supporting Parson Belin's work, Waccamaw Neck planters began encouraging their own Episcopal Church to bring Christian teachings to their slaves. Reverend Alexander Glennie of All Saints Episcopal Church later became well known for his missionary work among slaves and for the numerous slave chapels he convinced planters to build on the Waccamaw Neck. But it should not be forgotten that in the early years, it was Parson Belin who started this whole movement in our area. For many years, it was only he who brought the Christian Gospel to the slaves. He was the one who taught them hymns of the Methodist Church that they developed into their rich body of Gullah spirituals. He was the one who selected and developed Class Leaders, and even slave preachers, who became spiritual and political leaders of their people in the turbulent years that followed.

When Colonel Joshua John Ward bought Brookgreen Plantation from the Withers family in the 1830s, he encouraged Parson Belin and his assistants to continue working among his slaves.

So did Colonel Ward's son, Captain Joshua Ward, after he inherited Brookgreen and Springfield Plantations in the 1850s. (Of course Joshua Ward wasn't a Captain then; that came later when he took command of the Wachesaw Riflemen and then the Waccamaw Light Artillery during the War but I still think of him as Captain Ward and I'll call him that.)

Old Colonel Ward (and I can't tell you why he was called Colonel) had been a stern but fair master, respected by his slaves and the white community alike. Young Captain Joshua Ward continued this tradition. He and his wife Bessie were generally liked and respected by their workers. The plantations ran smoothly under his

Chapter 4

management and Class Leaders on them continued to be highly respected men among their fellow slaves and among planters.

Chapter 5.
The Great Sandy Island
Expedition

Like many young people in the 1950s and '60s, I was caught up in the revival of popular interest in folk music. My enjoyment of Kingston Trio records led to a curiosity about more authentic roots of our American folk tunes. I was so thrilled to receive a copy of the fascinating anthology, The Folk Songs of North America, by Alan Lomax, that I carried it everywhere with me, including to Murrells Inlet.

"You should show Miss Genevieve this book," Cousin Corrie suggested after I shared some entries with her. "I think she knows the man who wrote it."

I smiled indulgently at Cousin Corrie. In my young mind I couldn't conceive of our plain old Miss Genevieve as ever knowing anyone important enough to write such an impressive book.

Reluctantly, to humor Cousin Corrie, I brought the book with me the next time I visited Brookgreen Gardens.

I was right, of course. Miss Genevieve didn't know Alan Lomax at all. The man she knew was his father, John Lomax, the person responsible for the most important collection of American folk song and folklore recordings in the world today, the same John Lomax whose recordings and writings had fueled the entire folk song revival that so captured my interest!

I first got to know Mr. Lomax when I went to work for the WPA in the 1930s (Miss Genevieve explained). Our country went through a terrible Depression at that time. The prices of cotton and tobacco fell drastically here in South Carolina. People couldn't make a living farming and many lost their farms and their homes. The textile manufacturing plants closed too. So many people were out of work! And no welfare or Social Security to support them.

Mr. Roosevelt in Washington knew that something had to be done so he started all sorts of government programs as a part of his New Deal to put people back to work. One of the most important programs was the Works Projects Administration. A division of the WPA hired workers to build roads and parks and government buildings all over the country and then hired artists and craftsmen to decorate them, leaving us a marvelous legacy.

The part of the WPA that affected me was the Federal Writers' Project. My husband had died, leaving me with five young children to support. I was fortunate enough to get a position with the Federal Writers' Project because I had done some writing off and on over the years, mainly short pieces about our local culture for New York magazines.

Working for the WPA Writers' Project was one of the most interesting jobs I have ever held. Our best-known accomplishment was publishing the WPA Guide to South Carolina. Each state in the Union wrote a travel guide for that state that also included sections on its history, geography, economy, and culture. You can still find copies of these in many public libraries and they still make wonderful guides for exploring the states.

To me, an even more interesting WPA project involved writing up interviews with former slaves and collecting folktales and folk songs from them and from other local people. I got to know Mr. Lomax because he was Folklore Editor for the Federal Writers' Project. For years he had been collecting folk songs and stories from all over the South. He wanted to record traditional songs of local people before radio and phonograph records changed everything. When he read over the stories and songs I had collected, he recognized how alive the unique Gullah culture remained in our area.

Mr. Lomax and I corresponded regularly and he began including Murrells Inlet on his recording tours of the South. Fortunately, I was able to introduce him to a number of local people and persuade them to sing and tell stories into his recording equipment.

Mr. Lomax came to visit us here at Murrells Inlet several times over the years. He always brought his recording equipment and he usually brought his wife, who helped with the recording and kept notes on people and places he visited. She also tried to smooth over her husband's lack of social graces. Mr. Lomax was from Texas, don't you know. He talked like a cowboy and he acted like one too: kind of rough and not too civilized but very kind and friendly. The local people always remembered Mr. Lomax as that Texas cowboy who wanted to hear old time singing. Lots of people around here sang for him, both white people and black people.

Mr. Lomax had some fancy recording equipment owned by the Library of Congress, the government agency that sent him out to collect songs. When he could, he hooked up his recording equipment to electrical power but when that wasn't available he had big heavy batteries, sort of like our car batteries today, that could run the recording equipment for more than an hour. He carried it all, several hundred pounds worth, in the trunk of his Ford sedan.

Chapter 5

The recording machine itself looked a lot like a big bulky phonograph. There was a turntable and an arm with a needle attached to it. When he put a blank record on the turntable, set the needle on the disk, and turned the machine on, the record went around and around and the needle cut grooves in it recording the sound that came from the microphone. The microphone was a big box attached by wires to the recording machine. The wires were quite long so the singer and microphone did not have to be right by the recording machine.

Not all houses in this area had electricity at that time but the house where we lived with my father, the Hermitage, did, so Mr. Lomax often set up his recording equipment there. He would put the recording machine in the sitting room but would stretch the microphone wires out onto the porch where the singers preferred to perform because it was cooler there. He would operate the recording machine himself inside the house while Mrs. Lomax, outside, would announce the song or singer on the record and make sure they stood close enough to the microphone.

The records were 78s of course back then so there were only a few minutes of music on each side of the disk. Mr. and Mrs. Lomax had to carry boxes and boxes of records with them in the car in addition to the recording equipment and batteries, and their suitcases too of course. They were usually pretty heavily loaded when they pulled in to see me.

Mr. and Mrs. Lomax always spent time touring Brookgreen Gardens whenever they visited Murrells Inlet. Walking among the ancient live oak trees hung with Spanish moss was a special delight for them whether they came in summer when flowers were blooming or in winter when the Gardens were subdued in greens and grays.

When Mr. Lomax visited us here, it was always as part of a grand tour of several Southern states. The tours usually lasted a month or two as he visited Virginia, North Carolina, South Carolina, Georgia, Florida, Mississippi, Alabama, Texas, and maybe others. He usually stayed with us several days in Murrells Inlet. This was one of his main locations for Gullah, the creole language and culture developed by coastal Carolina slaves. Back then, lots of former slaves and their families still spoke Gullah, or at least understood it.

Those must have been adventurous expeditions for Mr. Lomax and his wife. They usually traveled along main highways and most of those, like the King's Highway, were paved by then but it was still a long way between towns if car trouble developed.

And it seemed like one thing or another was always interfering with his recordings—at least here in Murrells Inlet. One time, all the singers I had arranged for him to record got into some kind of family dispute and all refused to come sing for Mr. Lomax. I was able to find some other people to sing at the last minute but it was a confusion and he missed a lot of the songs I wanted him to record.

Another time, something was wrong with his recording needle and it had spoiled some disks. By the time he got to Murrells Inlet, he was down to his last few records and had to limit the number of songs he recorded.

One summer, there was a terrible polio epidemic in our area. Summers used to be dreadful that way. Thank goodness we don't have those anymore! That summer I had arranged to gather a group of local children together for Mr. Lomax to record play-party songs and rhymes, but then all gatherings of children were banned to try to control the spread of the disease. Once again, I had to find substitutes for the planned recordings.

Another visit presented a series of equally daunting obstacles at each turn but we managed to overcome them all and accomplish the most wonderful recordings of any of his visits, in my mind. We made some of these recordings in Murrells Inlet but we made some of these special recordings in a very special location. Today Brookgreen Gardens includes part of this unique place called Sandy Island.

Now Sandy Island isn't really on the Waccamaw Neck but it borders it. Here in Georgetown County, the Waccamaw River runs pretty much straight from north to south, parallel to the seacoast and only three or four miles inland, until it empties into Winyah Bay off Georgetown.

The Waccamaw Neck is that strip of land between the Waccamaw River and the ocean.

Well, about a mile farther inland from of the Waccamaw River, another river also runs north to south parallel to the Waccamaw River and also flows into Winyah Bay near Georgetown. This is the Pee Dee River. Along the whole length of where these two rivers run parallel to each other, little cross-streams connect the two rivers. The Waccamaw is a little lower than the Pee Dee so these little cross-streams drain water from the Pee Dee into the Waccamaw River all the way along. These two rivers are about the same size when they enter Georgetown County from the north but by the time they get to Winyah Bay, the Waccamaw is huge, more than a mile across, while the Pee Dee is pretty small, even though the Black River joins it just before it gets to the bay.

The cross-streams divide the swampy sandy land between the two rivers into islands, the biggest of which is Sandy Island. A good-sized cross-stream called Bull Creek (you remember, part of the Confederate trade routes) borders Sandy Island on its north end and a medium sized cross-stream called Thoroughfare Creek borders it on its south end. Of course, the Waccamaw borders it on the east side and the Pee Dee on the west side.

Sandy Island was always prime rice growing country. In fact, nine different rice plantations developed there, but most of the planters who owned them lived on the Waccamaw Neck or in

Chapter 5

Georgetown or Charleston. Sandy Island was isolated even in those days. Most slaves on Sandy Island were descendants of Africans who had been brought over in the 1700s. Very few slaves left Sandy Island and very few came from the outside in later years. The Gullah language and culture developed among slaves there until Gullah came to be the primary language spoken on Sandy Island, as on many plantations in the Lowcountry.

On Sandy Island before the War Between the States, Dr. Edward Heriot's Mont Arena Plantation, where the main river landing was located, became the center of activity. Dr. Heriot's friend, Captain Thomas Petigru, planted nearby Pipedown Plantation. Unlike most other men who owned plantations on Sandy Island, Dr. Heriot and Captain Petigru and their families actually lived there on their plantations.

Shortly before the War Captain Petigru died. His widow moved away and no longer wanted to operate Pipedown Plantation. She began looking for a buyer for the plantation and contacted several large landowners in the area but none was interested.

Pipedown slaves grew worried. They feared the Petigru family would abandon the plantation and send their slaves off to auction, separating them from their home and from each other.

So Sandy Island slaves took matters into their own hands in one of the few ways permitted to them by the laws of that time. In quite an unusual step, and one that demonstrated a unique level of independence and initiative, Pipedown slaves met together to select a new master for themselves! They discussed what they knew about each planter under consideration: the clothing, food, medical services, and religious opportunities he provided for his slaves; the type of overseers he hired; the disciplinary measures he used; and his history of buying and selling off slaves.

After much discussion, Pipedown slaves settled on Governor Robert Francis Withers Allston, who already owned lands on the Pee Dee River, to become their new master. Governor Allston was the son of Benjamin Allston who had inherited Brookgreen Plantation from his father, Gentleman Billy Allston, the Revolutionary War guerrilla fighter who married Rachel Moore, later Rachel Moore Allston Flagg. The Pipedown slaves all agreed that Governor Allston would make the best new master.

The next step was to convince Governor Allston! The Widow Petigru had already offered Pipedown and its slaves to Governor Allston but he had turned her down saying that he already owned more than enough land and slaves. (As it turned out, he was right, but that's another story.) So Sandy Islanders had quite a task ahead of them.

The community met again and selected Phillip Washington, the Pipedown Driver, to carry their request to Governor Allston. They chose Phillip Washington because he was intelligent and better educated than many of the other slaves. He was also well spoken and a leader respected by both his fellow slaves and by white planters.

The trip to Governor Allston was arranged. There Phillip Washington pleaded the case of the Pipedown slaves so eloquently that Governor Allston changed his mind, agreed to purchase Pipedown, and soon did so! The slaves of Pipedown had accomplished their goal. They had kept their community together and acquired themselves a new master of their own choosing.

~ ~ ~

The War caused disruptions on Sandy Island, as elsewhere, but very few slaves, or later, former slaves, left their homes there. For decades after Freedom Sandy Islanders maintained an isolated and independent community. They raised their own food and sold or traded rice for other necessities. The people of Sandy Island also preserved their Gullah culture and language like almost no other community. They kept their own customs and beliefs as well as their Gullah language long into the Twentieth Century.

Over the many years that I have been visiting Sandy Island I have gotten to know some of the islanders. One of the most interesting was Aunt Hagar Brown who lived here on the Waccamaw Neck but had close ties to Sandy Island. Aunt Hagar became one of my best and most enthusiastic informants when I was recording former slave narratives for the Federal Writers' Project in the 1930s.

When I told Mr. Lomax about Aunt Hagar and other Sandy Islanders, he was as excited as I was about making recordings of them telling their stories and singing their songs. Mr. Lomax and I corresponded several times about making sure Aunt Hagar and her people were available when he came to Murrells Inlet on his next recording trip. I assured him that I would have them ready to record.

My first obstacle, not entirely unexpected, was to get Aunt Hagar and the others to agree to meet and talk to Mr. Lomax. They talked readily to me about their life and their community but they weren't too sure they would have anything to say to this stranger. Outsiders, especially white men, and most especially white men from the government, rarely meant good news for Sandy Islanders.

Another obstacle to overcome with the Sandy Islanders was the idea of having their music and stories recorded. Most had heard music played from phonographs but some regarded these phonographs and phonograph records as instruments of the Devil. The whole idea of talking or singing into a record-making machine sounded suspicious to more than one.

After a good bit of talk on my part they finally agreed to meet Mr. Lomax but would make no promises from there on. I imagined that he would quickly make them feel comfortable and that everything would work out just fine. So I hadn't given the situation much more thought until a few days before Mr. Lomax was scheduled to arrive. Then I suddenly realized that I hadn't really thought through the logistics of getting Aunt Hagar, the Sandy Islanders, Mr. Lomax, and his equipment all together in the same place to make his recordings.

When I did start to consider this, my first thought was to have Aunt Hagar's people come over to the Hermitage for the day where we had electricity and could make our recordings with no trouble. That seemed like an easy and simple plan but Aunt Hagar soon put a stop to that notion. As much as she would like to please me and Mr. Lomax from Washington, her people had their own busy lives to tend to on Sandy Island and weren't about to pick up and leave them for anyone, especially under these strange circumstances!

What to do about this obstacle? The answer again seemed simple. We would just go over to Sandy Island to do the recording! After all, Mr. Lomax had batteries just so that he could record in places like that with no electricity.

Getting to Sandy Island was always easier said than done however. No roads ever connected Sandy Island to anyplace, and they still don't. The only way to get to Sandy Island is by boat.

Visiting Sandy Island usually took some hard rowing, even going and coming with the tide, whether from Wachesaw Landing or from the landing at Brookgreen. It had always been easy enough to find someone to take me though, but what was easy for me alone was not so easy when we needed to carry several people and several hundred pounds of recording equipment and batteries over the water. This was becoming quite an expedition!

Rowboats were easy to find but none of them was big enough and sturdy enough for our job. If Mr. Lomax had come during duck hunting season there would have been no difficulty at all. Yankee sportsmen up and down the river, like Mr. Kimbel at Wachesaw Plantation, had big comfortable cabin cruisers to take them out to hunting locations along the river. I'm sure they would have given us a ride. But it was summer and the boats were all stored away and most of the sportsmen had gone back up North. None of the workboats at Brookgreen Gardens was available either. Of course, there were several big powerful boats at docks in the salt-water creeks at Murrells Inlet but no easy way to get them around into the river.

I worried and fretted day and night over this obstacle. Mr. Lomax was already on his way to Murrells Inlet. Would I have to disappoint him? Finally, through a friend of Mr. Kimbel we were able to find some people down in Georgetown who thought it would make a lovely outing to bring their cabin cruiser upriver to Wachesaw Landing, spend a few nights at Murrells Inlet with friends, and transport us, our party, and our equipment over to Sandy Island for the day. What a relief! I could keep my promise to Mr. Lomax to record the Sandy Islanders!

By this point I was just waiting for the next obstacle to pop up. Yet everything went smoothly once Mr. Lomax arrived. I'm not sure Mr. Lomax had realized we would need to transport everything to Sandy Island by boat. And I know he was surprised when an oxcart met us at Mont Arena Landing to carry the recording machine, the records, the batteries, and our whole party up through the deeply rutted sand to Mont Arena Church where we set up the equipment. But he acted like it was the most natural thing in the world, traveling like this to get his recordings.

And the sessions with Aunt Hagar and the Sandy Islanders went beautifully. Mr. Lomax's friendly and informal ways were always quick to put people at ease. Once Aunt Hagar started talking, she went on and on. Others readily joined in, giving him much more than he had disks to record. He was able to record Aunt Hagar's stories about The Flagg Flood, some of her old-time songs from childhood, and answers to his inquiries about Sandy Island customs. His question about why door and window frames were painted blue ("To keep the evil spirits away!") even got her started on stories about haunts and hags and other supernatural creatures. Others added different songs and stories.

It was an extremely successful recording session and a perfectly delightful day for all of us. I don't think Mr. Lomax ever knew how much worry and effort I had put into making it happen. He just believed I could produce whatever he needed with a snap of my fingers, which was a good feeling for me.

So somewhere, carefully stored away in the Library of Congress with all the books ever printed in the United States, are the songs and stories of Aunt Hagar and her Sandy Island community, saved forever, just like we heard them that day on our Great Sandy Island Expedition. Maybe someday you will hear them too.

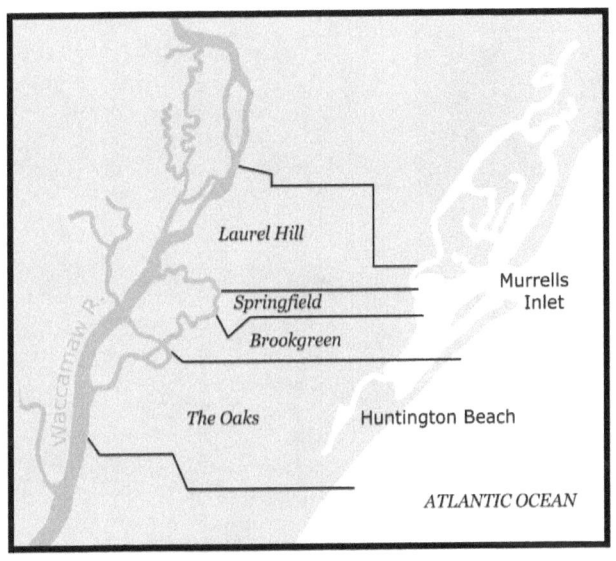

Plantations that became BrookgreenGardens

Chapter 6.
A Historical Note:
Phillip Washington,
Sandy Island Community
Organizer

Phillip Washington was one of the few freed slaves who left Sandy Island after the War. Although he was reluctant to leave his family and the home he loved, he was eager to explore new opportunities open to him as a free man. He moved to Georgetown where Federal occupation in the years following the War allowed former slaves possibilities for advancement in business and politics.

Phillip Washington became quite successful in business and even purchased a home on Front Street in the wealthiest section of Georgetown.

Racial tensions ran high however, and when occupying Federal forces finally left in 1877, whites regained their former power. They moved rapidly to undo opportunities former slaves had enjoyed during the previous ten years.

The native Sandy Islander quickly recognized the changing political and economic realities. He realized that he and others like him could no longer prosper in white society but he soon hit upon an alternative plan. He determined to found an independent self-sufficient community of former slaves back on his beloved Sandy Island.

Phillip Washington sold his house in Georgetown and moved back home to Sandy Island where he began establishing his community. First of all, he purchased a few acres of Mont Arena land and organized residents there to build a church, which soon became the spiritual and political center of the community. It remains so today. Next, he rented neighboring abandoned rice fields from struggling absentee planters and hired out of work former slaves to raise a rice crop. Fortunately the harvest was successful.

Phillip Washington used profits from that first rice crop and the rest of the proceeds from the sale of his house in Georgetown to purchase all of Mont Arena Plantation. With this as its base, his community of organized and resourceful former slaves on Sandy Island continued to thrive and prosper growing rice, even after Phillip Washington died around the turn of the century.

Early in the Twentieth Century, wealthy Yankees began buying up former rice plantations for hunting preserves, including other plantations

Chapter 6

on Sandy Island. After some negotiations, the Northern owners agreed to let Sandy Islanders raise rice on their newly acquired island preserves without paying rent. It was good for the duck hunting.

Sandy Island remains isolated to this day. There are still alligators there and strange plants like the insect-eating Venus Flytrap. Rare little Red-cockaded Woodpeckers still nest in hollows of ancient long leaf pines. Some even say that huge red headed Ivory billed Woodpeckers still live there although they are extinct most places. No white people have lived on Sandy Island, I imagine, since the last Heriot family members left shortly after the War.

Prince Washington, grandson of Phillip Washington, has become a community leader and now, in the middle of the Twentieth Century, is encouraging some modernization. School children have started riding a ferry across the river to come to school here on the mainland. Many of the adults have started commuting off the island to day jobs at Brookgreen Gardens or Pawley's Island or even at Myrtle Beach, especially as the tourist industry has grown, but they still don't have electricity or telephones on the island. It remains a unique place.

~

Have you enjoyed these
Lowcountry tales?

Please let others know about this book . . .

~ Loan it to a friend—or give copies to *all* your friends.

~ Mention it on Facebook, Twitter, blogs, etc.

~ Review it on Amazon, or on other websites such as Goodreads, LibraryThing, etc.

Thank you, in advance, for your assistance

Do you have questions or comments about
Gullah Ghosts?

Would you like to receive notice of
Lynn Michelsohn's new books
and special sales?

Contact her at:

2LynnMichelsohn@gmail.com

[You will receive no more than six notices a year. We *never* share your email address with anyone.]

Would you like to read more ghost stories and folktales from the South Carolina Lowcountry?

Lowcountry Ghosts

Stories of Alice Flagg, Confederate Blockade Runners, and Haunted Beads from South Carolina's Brookgreen Gardens

Tales from Brookgreen

Folklore, Ghost Stories, and Gullah Folktales in the South Carolina Lowcountry,

Includes all the stories from **Gullah Ghosts** and **Lowcountry Ghosts**, and *more*.

Both books are available in paperback and as ebooks.

Other Books
by Lynn Michelsohn

About the Galapagos Islands . . .

 *In the Galapagos Islands with Herman Melville*

Galapagos Islands Landscapes
(ebook only)

 *Galapagos Islands Birds*
(ebook only)

Herman Melville's The Chola Widow
(ebook only)

About Roswell, Santa Fe, and the Southwest . . .

Roswell
Your Travel Guide to the UFO
Capital of the World!

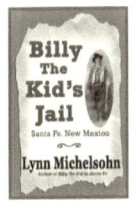

Billy the Kid's Jail
Santa Fe,
New Mexico

~ ~ ~

And writing for children, as Libby Lynn . . .

I See Santa Fe!
A Children's Guide

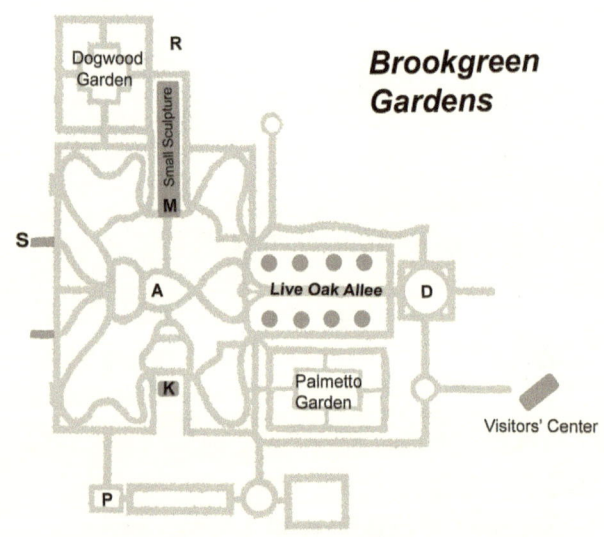

Brookgreen Gardens

Dogwood Garden

R

Small Sculpture

M

S

Live Oak Allee

A

D

K

Palmetto Garden

Visitors' Center

P

KEY

A = *Aligator Bender* Pool
D = *Diana* Pool
K = Old Kitchen
M = Former location of Museum

P = *Pegasus* Pool
R = Former location of Rest Rooms
S = Rice Island Steps

About the Storytellers
The Hostesses of
Brookgreen Gardens

One of my greatest treats as a child was to spend the day with Cousin Corrie at Brookgreen Gardens in Murrells Inlet, South Carolina. It was here in the warm Carolina Lowcountry that Archer and Anna Hyatt Huntington had created the first American sculpture garden among the ancient moss-draped live oak trees of four historic rice plantations: Brookgreen, Springfield, Laurel Hill, and The Oaks.

In those simpler days, visitors to Brookgreen Gardens turned off the narrow pavement of Highway 17, the King's Highway, onto two parallel ribbons of concrete spaced far enough apart to support the wheels of a car. Visitors drove slowly along those concrete ribbons through the wooded deer park and past the island of Youth Taming the Wild to a sandy parking lot near the Diana Pool. There they left their cars in as shady a spot as possible and entered the Gardens on foot, with no admission fee or gatekeeper.

GULLAH GHOSTS

After a leisurely stroll through the Live Oak Allee, with perhaps a detour into the Palmetto Garden, a peek inside the Old Kitchen, and a dip of the fingers into the cool water of the Alligator Bender Pool, visitors arrived at the low wide porch of a simple gray-brick building. This structure had once housed the overseer when Brookgreen was a thriving rice plantation. Now it served as the Museum and the entranceway to two open-air galleries for small sculpture. Inside the Museum, steady sounds of splashing water from the Frog Baby Fountain in the first gallery created a feeling of sanctuary from summer heat that grew oppressive by mid-morning in the Lowcountry.

This Museum was the Visitors' Center of its day. Here two "sixty-ish" Southern ladies in sturdy shoes welcomed visitors. These two Hostesses were the only staff in evidence throughout the Gardens, other than the occasional groundskeeper trimming ivy. In the cool dim interior of the Museum, Miss Genevieve and Cousin Corrie sold postcards, gave directions, and told stories to visitors interested enough to ask questions about the Gardens.

Boxy glass display cases formed a counter along the front wall of the Museum. Mostly, these cases held stacks of picture postcards. Black-and-white cards sold for five cents, sepia cards for ten cents, and colored cards for twenty-five cents each. Books and pamphlets about the Gardens were also available. Intermixed with this literature stood other items, not for sale, that stimulated frequent questions and often led to Miss Genevieve and Cousin Corrie's stories.

Cousin Corrie, my first cousin one generation removed, was born Cornelia Sarvis Dusenbury in 1888 as her home state of South Carolina emerged from the chaos of Reconstruction. She spent much of her childhood at Murrells Inlet on the Carolina coast and then worked for many years as a schoolteacher and librarian in Florence, South Carolina. In retirement Cousin Corrie returned to Murrells Inlet and joined Genevieve Wilcox Chandler, a writer, artist, and local historian, to become a Hostess at Brookgreen Gardens.

Miss Genevieve was just a bit younger than Cousin Corrie. She had come to Murrells Inlet with her family from Marion, South Carolina but stayed, married, and raised five children here. She often supported them by writing articles on local subjects after the early death of her husband. When the Huntingtons created Brookgreen Gardens they asked Miss Genevieve to become its Hostess.

During my visits to Brookgreen Gardens, Cousin Corrie and Miss Genevieve (as I called her, using the traditional Southern form of address for a grown-up family friend) let me help them with their hostess duties, much to my delight. I also enjoyed playing hide-and-seek among sun-dappled sculptures and looking for painted river turtles sleeping on logs that floated in the old rice field swamps. I loved darting from the shelter of one live oak canopy to the next during summer showers. I especially thrilled at wading in out-of-the-way sculpture pools when no one was looking. But my very favorite activity was listening to Miss Genevieve and Cousin Corrie tell stories of Brookgreen and the Carolina Lowcountry to spellbound Garden visitors, me included.

Each Hostess had her own distinct repertoire. One never encroached on the other's territory. "Now you will have to ask Mrs. Chandler about that," or "Miss Dusenbury can tell you that story," were common responses to visitors' queries. If one or the other of the ladies were absent that day, then the unlucky visitor left without hearing her special tales.

Miss Genevieve tended to cover historical figures and folktales. She had collected local stories for "Mr. Roosevelt" and the 1930s WPA. Cousin Corrie focused on hurricanes, family tales, and accounts of Confederate and Yankee conflicts on the Carolina coast. Her stories related more to her own personal experiences. Of course each had her own unique collection of ghost stories.

I heard some of these stories repeated to countless visitors. The tale of the haunted Wachesaw beads was a frequent favorite. Other stories I only heard once or twice and remember only in snippets, although I have often been able to fill in gaps from other sources. All these stories excited my interest in the historical figures and everyday people who came here before us to the broad rice fields and wooded uplands that became Brookgreen Gardens.

These are stories Miss Genevieve and Cousin Corrie told, as best I remember them. In my mind these tales weave themselves together with swaying Spanish moss, sparkling splashing fountains, and winding gray-brick latticework of Brookgreen Gardens to create visions of a timeless spirit forever living in the heart of the Carolina Lowcountry.

About the Author

Charles Town blacksmith William Green purchased his first land near that new Carolina settlement in 1695. His descendents have continued to live and thrive in the Carolina Lowcountry for more than three hundred years.

Lynn Michelsohn, one of William Green's ninth-generation granddaughters, was born not too far away in Durham, North Carolina. She grew up steeped in Lowcountry stories, as well as in the black mud of its tidal marshes. Her heart remains among the moss-draped live oaks lining the saltwater creeks of South Carolina's Waccamaw Neck. Now, she and her husband have two sons who love the Lowcountry almost as much as she does.

In these tales, this native Carolinian retells stories she heard from two early hostesses at Brookgreen Gardens: Mrs. Genevieve Wilcox Chandler and the author's cousin, Miss Corrie Dusenbury. Through these stories she conveys her sense of romance, history, and mystery hidden just beneath the serenely beautiful surface of Brookgreen Gardens, one of South Carolina's most popular tourist attractions.

The author

as she was . . .

. . . and remains always

. . . in her heart

A Selection from . . .

Lowcountry Ghosts

Genevieve Wilcox Chandler, one of the hostesses at South Carolina's Brookgreen Gardens in the middle of the Twentieth Century, told this story about Wachesaw ghosts at an Indian burial ground excavation in Murrells Inlet, South Carolina in the 1930s . . .

"I won't die for a few teeth and arrowheads. No, I won't," muttered James. Staring at the ground, he placed a bundle wrapped in a croaker sack at the feet of the archeologist supervising the dig.

The subdued laborer continued, his voice louder but his haunted eyes remaining downcast, "Boss, I've come to confess."

The archeological dig where James worked had caused a lot of excitement around here that summer. Local workers, who were used to finding occasional arrowheads or broken pieces of pottery in the pinelands or along the beach, were not impressed with the finds at first. Their biggest concern appeared to be their uneasiness in digging up bones. Many would not work on the project because they believed that graves, whether white, black, or Indian, should never be disturbed. So it was only to be expected that when archeological work began, great distress arose among the local people that graves were being excavated.

Warnings of dire happenings were whispered from person to person. Stories circulated about loud wailings from Wachesaw Bluff echoing through the night. None of us ever heard any wailing, and I'm not sure what local people would have gotten close enough to the diggings at night to hear such wailings, but the stories grew. Every sickness and stubbed toe was blamed on disturbing the dead.

Many would not help with the excavations. Those who did must have been less fearful of the supernatural world, or been in greater need of the excellent wages paid by the museum scientists.

The men who did work soon caught the enthusiasm and excitement the archeologists displayed at each new discovery. The scientists' excitement over a cache of small beads or a shell bracelet or a chipped stone ax quickly created awe among the workers for each seemingly plain object. There was much talk of how "valuable" each piece was. Of course, the scientists were referring to the value of knowledge about the past that each item imparted. No one realized workers had begun to believe that these items had great monetary value. They only began to understand as they listened to James' unusual story.

~ ~ ~

Once James understood how valuable the artifacts were (he explained) it was hard to resist pocketing just a few. He had grinned to himself thinking about selling them for much-needed cash or supplies. He knew he would have to take them to a big town to make any real money but figured his brother, who worked for the railroad in Florence, could help the next time he came home on a visit.

Soon James had quite a collection of relicts in his small cabin: arrowheads, handfuls of beads, and several small axes. He had also collected a pocketful of odd-looking loose teeth. These he kept in a coffee can on his mantel.

James felt bad about taking objects but tried to look at it just as extra pay for a job no one else had the courage to take on. He also reasoned that money from the artifacts would be much more important to him than to Mr. Kimbel who owned the property. He already had more money than anyone needed!

Still, James' conscience bothered him and he didn't sleep well at night even though he was tired from the excavation work. Tossing and turning one night, he gradually realized that way off in the distance he could hear the wailing voices that everybody talked about, or was it just wind in the pines? Each successive night he slept more poorly, between worrying about his stealing (because that was what he was having to admit he was doing) and listening for wailing or other strange noises outside in the night.

One night the noises were no longer outside. They came from inside the cabin, right there with James! He awoke to rattling sounds from the coffee can on his mantel and strange low murmurs from shadows passing in front of the window. As James lay stark still, the noises grew fainter and the sound of his pounding heart grew louder. By the time the sun came up, he had convinced himself that he had just had a bad dream.

Still, it was even harder to get to sleep the next night and close to morning James again awakened with a start to the same rattling noises and moving shadows, only this time their voices were louder and their tone was angry. He could not make out any words but the shadows were clearly men and it looked like they were waving weapons at him! Fear clutched his heart. He could hardly breathe, much less move. The next thing James knew, sun was streaming in the window. Relieved to be awake, alive, and away from his horrible nightmare, he headed out to another day of digging.

That night James lay down to sleep with increasing trepidation in spite of his increasing exhaustion. Distant thunder signaled a building storm. In spite of his fears, James quickly fell asleep. A clap of thunder soon woke him to a frightening spectacle however.

Flashing lightning illuminated a group of angry Indian braves decked out in skins and feathers there in the room with him, shaking their spears and tomahawks at him! Frozen with fear, James could hear chanting and shouting as well as rattling and pounding, even over the thunderclaps. The Indian braves stomped and gestured directly at him ever more wildly!

Suddenly a gigantic flash of lightning and a thunderous crash shook the cabin! In that flash the braves in their regalia vanished but the coffee can hurtled off the mantel, scattering teeth all across the floor.

James sat bolt upright in bed, terrified. Thunder and lightning continued but the braves never returned. James lit a lamp and sat up the remainder of the night, wide-awake, but he was not visited again.

At dawn, James bundled up the artifacts, getting down on his hands and knees to search out every last tooth from under his sparse furniture. He took the bundle straight to the dig and presented it, along with his confession, to the scientist in charge that morning.

James begged to be allowed to continue working on the dig because he was in great need of money. The scientist accepted his confession, along with the return of the stolen items, and agreed to let James keep working. Here was one worker who certainly wasn't going to carry off any more artifacts!

The excavations continued in the Carolina Lowcountry—but so did the mysterious happenings . . .

Lowcountry Ghosts

(available in paperback or as an ebook)

~ ~ ~

Thank you for reading this selection. We hope you will continue to enjoy her writings.

Happy Reading!